Personal Finance Boot Camp

Camp

Ten Steps to Mastering Your Wealth

Table of Contents

Chapter 1. Introduction

Step into the exciting world of financial empowerment with our Special Report entitled, "Personal Finance Boot Camp: Ten Steps to Mastering Your Wealth." This comprehensive and approachable guide serves as your personal finance coach, leading you through a structured program designed to help you conquer your financial goals. You don't have to be an economist to get your finances in shape—you just need the right training! With ten concrete steps, we'll turn seemingly insurmountable money mountains into manageable molehills. Equipping yourself with this guide is like investing in your powerhouse of financial wisdom. Are you ready to take back control, boost your financial confidence, and stride toward a secure future? Your journey to mastering your wealth begins here. Together, let's build the prosperous life you've been dreaming of!

Chapter 2. Understanding Your Personal Finance Landscape

Before we begin sculpting your new budget or designing an investment strategy, it's critical to comprehend your existing financial situation. Knowing where you stand financially is the first step to creating a successful personal finance plan. This knowledge gives you a roadmap to guide your financial decisions and helps you avoid potential pitfalls. In this chapter, we'll delve deeply into how to understand and navigate your current personal finance landscape.

2.1. The Importance of Financial Insight

Understanding your personal finance landscape is as crucial as having a clear roadmap before embarking on a long journey. It's the initial step towards financial prosperity, which ultimately leads to financial independence and security. Your financial landscape, in its simplest form, is a snapshot of your financial health.

It includes knowing your income, understanding your expenses, identifying your debts, being aware of your savings, and having a pulse on your investments. This information provides vital insights into your assets, liabilities, and cash flows, helping you make informed financial decisions. It depicts your financial strengths and weaknesses, paving the way to capitalize on opportunities and mitigate risks.

2.2. Analyzing Your Income

Your income is the primary source of your financial power—it fuels your savings, investments, and expenditures. However, your income isn't just your monthly paycheck; it comprises various sources.

You can categorize your income into two types: active and passive. Active income is what you earn by trading your time, like from your 9 to 5 job or a freelance gig. Passive income, on the other hand, is money you earn that doesn't require your routine involvement, such as dividends from your investments or rental income.

Look at all sources of income and exactly how much each one contributes. This step is as simple as reviewing your payslips, bank statements, dividend checks, or rental agreements. Record your income accurately to better understand your financial power.

2.3. Managing Your Expenditures

Now that we have a handle on income, let's look at your spending. Your expenses give you valuable insights into where your money is going each month. Understanding your spending patterns can expose certain tendencies and habits, essential for devising a sustainable budget and savings plan.

Divide your expenses into two categories: fixed and variable. Fixed expenses include your mortgage/rent, car payments, insurance premiums, and similar obligations that generally don't change from month to month. Variable expenses include entertainment, groceries, dining out, and other expenses that fluctuate.

Review your bank and credit card statements to see where your money goes. Use a spreadsheet or budget management app to keep track.

2.4. Discerning Your Debts

Debt can be a considerable burden, consuming your income and depleting your ability to save and invest. It's crucial to detail all your debts, like credit cards, student loans, auto loans, and mortgages. List each one with its associated interest rate, minimum payments, and total balance.

Understanding your debts offers clarity into the gravity of their effects on your financial landscape. This information is critical in devising a repayment strategy that reduces interest payments and eliminates debt quickly.

2.5. Gauging Your Savings and Investments

Your savings and investments represent your financial resilience and your ability to grow wealth. Look at all of your savings accounts, emergency funds, retirement accounts, and other investments.

Savings provide you a financial cushion against emergencies, sudden income loss, or unforeseen expenses. Investments, meanwhile, help your wealth grow over time to achieve long-term financial goals.

It's crucial to understand how much you're saving and how your investments are performing. Monitor these metrics regularly to ensure they align with your financial objectives.

2.6. Your Personal Financial Statement

With the understanding of income, expenses, debts, savings, and investments, you can now compile your personal financial statement—an essential tool in the mastery of personal finance. This statement, like those used by businesses, provides a consolidated view of your financial health.

To create your statement, list all of your assets (what you own) and liabilities (what you owe). Subtract your liabilities from your assets to get your net worth. This number gives you a baseline to measure the progress of your financial wellness and the effectiveness of your financial strategies.

Remember, understanding your personal finance landscape is a vital first step towards financial mastery. It's like standing on a hilltop, looking out over your terrain, and planning your route. Now, cognizant of your financial circumstance, you can make confident decisions and stride assuredly toward your prosperous future.

Chapter 3. Setting Clear and Achievable Financial Goals

Building a stable and secure financial foundation demands defining and setting clear, tangible and achievable goals. This necessitates understanding what you want from your financial life. These aspirations act as guideposts, helping you cement your financial planning, budgeting, and investing strategies. Let's delve into the essentials of setting clear and achievable financial goals.

3.1. Why Set Financial Goals

The first step towards achieving financial control is identifying the reasons behind starting your monetary adventure. Financial goals guide your budgeting and investment decisions, aligning them to your future and present aspirations that are personal to you, thereby making every financial decision impactful and meaningful.

Here are some reasons why setting explicit financial goals is paramount:

1. Direction: To forge a path towards financial stability, you need a clear-cut direction. Setting well-defined goals guides your financial actions and gives you a 'north star' when you veer off-track.

2. Motivation: Goals give you something to work towards. They motivate you to take the right steps and maintain financial discipline.

3. Empowerment: Clear goals empower you to take control of your financial journey by making you responsible for your own financial growth and success.

4. Result-Oriented: Goals translate your lofty aspirations into actionable steps, making your journey less daunting and more

oriented towards achievable results.

3.2. Elements of Clear and Achievable Financial Goals

Crafting efficient financial goals involves more than just a wish list. They should be SMART - Specific, Measurable, Achievable, Relevant, and Time-bound. Each word in this acronym provides an important characteristic of a successful goal, and mastering them can significantly affect your probability of success.

1. **Specific:** Clearly describe what you want to achieve. A goal like "save more money" is ambiguous. A more specific goal would be, "save $10,000 for a down payment on a house."

2. **Measurable:** Have a metric to track and measure your progress. Using the above example, you can measure the progress by checking how close you are to the $10,000 mark.

3. **Achievable:** The goal must be attainable considering your income, expenses, and lifestyle. If you earn $50,000 a year, setting a goal to save $50,000 in a year may be unrealistic.

4. **Relevant:** Your goal should resonate with your broader financial objectives and life circumstances. If you're planning to buy a house, saving for a down payment is a relevant goal.

5. **Time-bound:** State when you wish to reach the goal. Giving yourself a deadline creates a sense of urgency and helps track progress over time.

3.3. Setting Short-Term, Medium-Term, and Long-Term Goals

Understanding financial timelines is significant, as not all goals are targeted for the same timeframe. Broadly, they can be categorized into three:

1. **Short-Term Goals (within a year):** These are immediate goals that you wish to achieve within a year. It could be repaying a small debt, saving for a vacation, or creating an emergency fund.

2. **Medium-Term Goals (1 to 5 years):** These are goals that require a little more time and planning. E.g., saving for a down payment on a house or car.

3. **Long-Term Goals (more than 5 years):** These goals require a lot of patience and consistent effort. They normally involve life-altering events like saving for a child's education, paying off mortgage, or planning for retirement.

Setting goals for different timelines can help balance your financial aspirations with your current living standards, ensuring that you're not compromising today for a distant future or vice versa.

3.4. Creating a Goal-Based Budget

Your budget is the financial roadmap that leads you towards your goal. Goal-based budgeting lets you prioritize your spending around your defined objectives.

A goal-based budget involves the following steps:

1. **Income:** Identify your total monthly income from all sources.

2. **Expenses:** Categorize your expenses into necessary (rent, utilities, groceries) and discretionary (dining out, entertainment).

3. **Financial Goals:** Allocate a portion of your income to meet each financial goal.

4. **Remaining Income:** Divide what's left into savings, investments, and recreation.

Remember, budgeting should keep you financially healthy without depriving you of your lifestyle. Finding a balance is key.

3.5. Overcoming Obstacles

Roadblocks are inevitable in your financial journey. Changes in income, unexpected expenditures, or market shifts may slow your progress. It's crucial to regularly review and adapt your financial plan to overcome these hurdles.

The trick to overcoming these obstacles is to anticipate the unexpected. Build an emergency fund as a safety net for unexpected expenses, ensure a good health and life insurance cover, and diversify your investments to spread risk.

Remember, setting clear and achievable financial goals is not a one-time event. It's an ongoing, dynamically evolving process that mirrors your life's progression. Consistency, regular reviews and updates, discipline, and persistence are the building blocks of this voyage towards a secure financial future. The journey might seem intimidating initially, but the reward of financial security and freedom is a treasured one. So stride fearlessly towards your goal. The prosperous life you've been dreaming of is waiting at the end.

Chapter 4. Mapping Your Income and Expense

In your journey to financial empowerment, one of the first critical steps is to understand and map your income and expenses. This part of the process serves as the foundation upon which you can build your financial goals.

4.1. Understand Your Income

The primary step to financial mastery is understanding your income. This is not merely about knowing the amount that hits your bank account at the end of the month. It's about understanding the various streams of income that you have, how stable they are, and how they might change in the future.

Primarily, there are two types of income: active and passive. Active income is where you actively have to do something to receive remuneration. Examples of active income include your regular day job, your side business, or a part-time gig. On the other hand, passive income is money you earn regularly with little or no ongoing effort. It usually involves an initial investment of time or money, such as rental income, interest or dividends, or affiliate marketing.

Use the table below to map your streams of income:

Income Stream	Type of Income (Active / Passive)	Amount ($)	Frequency	Stability (High / Moderate / Low)
Job title / Property etc.	Active / Passive	$$$	Weekly / Monthly / Annually	High / Moderate / Low

I encourage you to write down every income source, including the irregular ones. This comprehensive view will set the foundation for the next steps.

4.2. Detail Your Expenses

After understanding income, the next task is detailing your expenses. While it could be mentally taxing to think about where your money is going, having a clear snapshot is essential for effective financial management.

Expenses typically fall into three categories: fixed, variable, and discretionary. Fixed expenses are those that remain constant every month, such as your rent or mortgage. Variable expenses fluctuate monthly, like utilities or gasoline. Discretionary expenses represent non-essential spending—things like dining out, vacations, hobbies, and entertainment.

Identify your expenses and categorize them using the table below:

Expense Category	Fixed / Variable / Discretionary	Amount ($)	Frequency
Rent / Utilities / Entertainment etc.	Fixed / Variable / Discretionary	$$$	Weekly / Monthly / Annually

4.3. Analyzing Your Income and Expenses

Once you've listed your income and expenses, it's time to scrutinize these figures. Compare your total income against your total expenses. Are you living within your means, or spending more than you make? If your expenses exceed your income, it's an immediate call to action.

But even if you're breaking even or somewhat saving, you should still aim to optimize your financial habits.

4.4. Expense Optimization

Analyzing your expenses might reveal areas where you're overspending. Perhaps your discretionary spending is higher than you realized. Or maybe you discover some 'money leaks'—spending on things you don't actually need or value. Start to prioritize your expenses and align them with your financial goals. Remember, even small adjustments to day-to-day choices can make a significant impact over time.

4.5. Setting Up a Buffer

It's wise to remember that life is unpredictable and circumstances can change. Changes in the job market, health incidents, or unexpected expenses can occur at any moment. Hence, as a part of this financial mapping, you should aim to set up an 'emergency buffer'. Financial experts normally recommend this to be anywhere from 3 to 6 months' worth of expenses.

4.6. Adopt Balance

While managing finances, it's essential to strike a balance. Restricting yourself too much might cause resentment and frustration, setting you up for failure in your financial journey. It's essential to occasionally splurge, plan for vacations, and enjoy your earnings while also ensuring a secure future.

By taking the time to map your income and expenses, you've begun the process of gaining control over your financial life. In the chapters to follow, we will delve deep into how you can leverage this understanding to save effectively, invest wisely, and ultimately master your wealth. Let this chapter be a strong foundation upon which you construct your financial fortress.

Chapter 5. Demystifying the World of Taxes

Taxation might appear a daunting subject— a maze of percentages, legal jargon, and unending paperwork. However, with a proper understanding, you can navigate this world successfully, fully grasping the implications of your financial decisions and how they impact your tax liabilities. We'll begin with the fundamentals to build a robust foundation of comprehension.

5.1. Basic Concepts of Taxation

In it's simplest form, a tax is a compulsory payment levied by the government on incomes, goods, services, or activities. It's a pivotal source of revenue for the government, used to fund various public goods and services. While the specifics often vary across jurisdictions, tax systems share certain fundamental elements:

- **Taxpayer**: The entity responsible for paying the tax. They could be individuals, businesses, or other organizations.

- **Tax Base**: The total amount of income, property, or consumption subject to taxation.

- **Tax Rate**: The rate at which the tax base is taxed. For income taxes, progressive tax systems apply varying tax rates based on income levels.

Understanding these key concepts lays the groundwork for demystifying this complex system.

5.2. Understanding Different Types of Taxes

We face a variety of taxes in our everyday lives. Breaking them down can help make them manageable:

1. **Income Tax**: Levied on personal and business income, after applying certain exemptions and deductions.

2. **Sales Tax**: Applied to goods and services at the point of purchase.

3. **Property tax**: Based on the value of owned property like land and buildings.

4. **Capital Gains Tax**: Imposed on profits from the sale of an investment or real estate.

5.3. Demystifying the Income Tax

The income tax is perhaps the most pervasive and intricate tax. It is levied directly on your yearly earnings from employment, investment interest, dividends, sale of assets, and other income streams. Different income sources can have varying tax implications, making it crucial to understand its nuances.

Income tax calculation involves deductions and exemptions. Deductions are subtractions from your gross income for specific expenditures like retirement savings contributions or medical costs. Exemptions, on the other hand, represent portions of your income that are not subjected to tax. They're typically accorded based on taxpayer characteristics like family size or disability status. After deductions and exemptions are applied, the remaining amount—your taxable income—determines your tax liability.

5.4. Understanding Tax Brackets

Income tax rates vary across income levels, forming what is known as 'tax brackets'. The US, for instance, employs seven federal tax brackets ranging from 10% to 37%. It's important to note that these rates are marginal, meaning that they apply to each portion of your income within the respective tax band, not your total income.

5.5. Calculating Your Tax

To calculate your tax, you start by determining your gross income, apply any deductions, and then calculate the amount of tax due at each applicable tax bracket. This figure is your initial tax liability. From this, you would then subtract any tax credits—dollar-for-dollar reductions—that you're eligible for. The result is your final tax liability.

5.6. Navigating Tax Forms and Documentation

To file your taxes, you need to understand the necessary forms and their purposes. In the US, individuals typically file their income tax returns using one of three forms: Form 1040, Form 1040A, or Form 1040EZ. Form selection is based on factors like taxable income, filing status, and eligibility for credits.

Keeping reliable records is vital for accurate tax filing and verification if audited. Organize all relevant documents, receipts, and forms, including W-2s from your employer and 1099s for other income sources.

5.7. Making Sense of the Sales Tax

Sales taxes are typically state-level taxes imposed on the sale of goods and services. The consumer pays the tax, but the business collecting it is responsible for remitting it to the government. While most states impose sales taxes, rates and rules can significantly vary between them.

Sales taxes generally apply at the point of sale as a percentage of the sales price. Some goods, like essential food items, can be exempted from the tax or taxed at lower rates in some jurisdictions to reduce the burden on low-income individuals.

5.8. Deciphering Property Tax

Property taxes are annual levies on property owners based on an assessed value of their property. The tax amount is often a percentage, known as a mill rate, applied to the appraised value. Local governments typically use revenues from property taxes to fund services like education, transportation, and public safety.

5.9. Unravelling the Capital Gains Tax

Capital gains tax applies to the profit made from selling an investment or real estate. The tax rate varies based on how long you own the asset before selling. If you hold the asset for over a year before selling, it's considered a long-term capital gain and typically has a lower tax rate than ordinary income.

Understanding and managing taxes is a crucial element of financial empowerment. It not only helps us meet our legal responsibilities but also equips us with the knowledge to optimize our taxable income and ensure our financial decisions are tax-efficient. As you progress in your financial journey, consider tapping into professional tax advice to help you further minimize your tax liabilities and leverage tax benefits.

Chapter 6. Mastering the Art of Budgeting

Understanding, creating, and maintaining a budget is a timeless pillar of personal finance. It's the foundation upon which you build your financial goals. Hence, this chapter seeks to guide you on how to master the art of budgeting in a comprehensive, approachable manner that will turn budgeting into a daily financial victory, rather than a chore.

6.1. Why Budgeting Matters

Budgeting is the process of creating a plan for your money. It ensures that you will have enough for the things you need and the items that are most important to you. A budget helps you keep track of your spending and make informed decisions throughout the month. If you're trying to save money, pay off debt, or just better understand where your money goes, a budget is a powerful tool that can help you reach those goals.

Budgeting empowers you to control your finances. It enhances your awareness of your income and helps you understand how it gets distributed to different expense categories. It also helps you avoid overspending on non-essential items, thus keeping your financial health in check.

6.2. Creating Your Budget

The first step in mastering the art of budgeting is to create your plan. The crucial elements necessary for an efficient budgeting plan include:

1. Your total income: This includes your salary, any tips, bonuses,

income from side jobs, dividends, etc.

2. Your fixed expenses: These are the costs that do not change from month to month. This could include your rent or mortgage payments, car payments, utility bills, and insurance premiums.

3. Your variable expenses: These are costs that might change every month such as groceries, gas, entertainment, dining out, etc.

Here are detailed steps to help you create your budget:

1. Calculate Your Income: Tally up every reliable income source you have. Ensure you only count net income – the income remaining after all deductions like taxes, social security, etc.

2. Itemize Your Expenses: Track all your expenses for a month or two to understand how much you spend and where you spend it. Use receipts, bank statements, and credit card statements to help distinguish between your fixed and variable costs.

3. Set Your Financial Goals: Knowing what you're budgeting for gives purpose and motivation to your budgeting routine. Your goals could include saving for a down payment on a house, building an emergency fund, paying off debt, or saving for retirement.

4. Tailor Your Budget: Use your income and expenses to create a budget that aligns with your goals. Start by allocating money to your fixed costs, then to your variable expenses. The balance should go towards your savings or be used to pay down debt.

5. Implement Your Budget: Use a budgeting tool or app to help you stick to your plan. Regularly update your budget, adjusting figures as necessary. Budgeting is a dynamic process that changes as your life and financial situation change.

6.3. Strategies to Stick to Your Budget

Sticking to your budget might be challenging, particularly in the early stages. Here are some strategies to aid adherence:

1. Automate savings: With financial technology, it's easier than ever to automate your savings. This way, you are less tempted to overspend your savings.

2. Cut back on non-essentials: Luxury, entertainment, and other non-essential spendings might need to be reduced to meet your financial goals.

3. Spend with a purpose: Avoid impulse buying. Think before you spend.

4. Track Expenses: Keep an eye on where your money is going by regularly checking your bank and credit card statements.

6.4. Reviewing and Adjusting Your Budget

Over time, it's inevitable that your budget will require adjustments. Your income may change, your expenses may fluctuate, and your financial goals will evolve. To keep your budget relevant:

1. Review Your Budget Regularly: Schedule monthly (or at least quarterly) budget reviews to identify areas where you're overspending, not saving enough, or otherwise veering from your financial plan.

2. Adjust as Needed: If you find an area in your budget that's consistently problematic, address it directly. If your budget isn't working for you, change it.

3. Celebrate Small Victories: Reaching small milestones can give a

tremendous boost to your financial morale. It helps you keep up the momentum.

While mastering the art of budgeting might seem daunting at the outset, with patience, consistency, and a little planning, it can become a significant aspect of your financial empowerment journey. Remember, a budget is not a restriction on your money, but a plan for it. Every budget has a purpose: to provide you with the freedom to spend wisely and enjoy life while achieving your financial goals.

By mastering the art of budgeting, you are unlocking the first level of financial freedom. It's a critical stride towards feeling confident about your money matters and building the prosperous life you've been dreaming of. Now that you are armed with this knowledge and guidance, you are on your way to becoming a budgeting master.

Chapter 7. Smart Saving Strategies

Whether you're working to pay off debts, saving for a retirement, or putting money aside for a dream vacation, saving money is a universal necessity. As simple as it may sound, effective saving strategies can be quite complex. Here, we explore various ways to make your savings work best for your unique financial situation.

7.1. Understand Your Saving Goals

First and foremost, it is crucial to identify what you are saving for. This will not only keep you motivated, but will also help determine the best strategies for you. Do you want to save for retirement, a down payment on a house, your children's education, or for an emergency fund? Once you know your goals, it's easier to plan the path towards achieving it.

7.2. Creating a Budget

The backbone of any solid savings plan begins with creating a budget. Here's how.

1. Analyze Current Spending: Start by tracking your daily spending habits for a few weeks or months. This will give you a clear picture of where your money is going.

2. Categorize Expenses: Divide your expenses into categories such as rent, groceries, utilities, entertainment, dining out, etc. Decide which are necessities and which are luxuries you can limit.

3. Allocate Funds: Set a spending limit for each category, focusing on reducing the non-essential categories. Remember, the goal is to put an end to wasteful expenditures and channel that money

into savings.

4. Regularly Review and Tweak the Budget: Regularly review and adjust your budget as necessary. Financial situations can change rapidly, and so should your budget.

7.3. Automating Savings

Thanks to modern banking technologies, you can make saving a lot easier by automating your savings. Here are the steps to set this up:

1. Open a High-Yield Savings Account: Use this account exclusively for your emergency fund or savings goal.

2. Set Up Direct Deposit: If your employer offers direct deposit, have a portion of each paycheck automatically deposited into your high-yield savings account.

3. Regular Review: Just as with your budget, regularly review your automated savings strategy and adjust as necessary based on your financial situation.

7.4. Eliminating Debt

In many cases, the best way to pave the way for savings is to eliminate outstanding debt.

7.5. Investing for the Future

Develop a Snowball or Avalanche Payment Strategy: Snowball strategy involves starting with the smallest debt and working your way up, while the avalanche approach focuses on tackling the highest-interest debt first.

Investing can be a powerful way to grow your savings. Compounding interest can turn a small investment now into significant savings down the line. While investing always comes with risks, a well-planned and diversified investment portfolio can yield substantial gains.

1. Retirement Accounts: If you're not already contributing to a retirement account, start now. If you're employed, take advantage of employer-matched retirement plans such as 401(k) to make the most of your savings.

2. Brokerage Accounts: If you have savings in addition to your retirement contributions, consider opening a brokerage account. This allows you to invest in stocks, bonds, mutual funds and more.

3. Cryptocurrency: It's a newer form of investing, and not for everyone. However, with careful consideration and research, investing a small portion of your savings in cryptocurrency could reap returns down the line.

While these strategies are not exhaustive, they provide an excellent starting point for anyone seeking to master their wealth. Money management skills, like any other, can be cultivated over time with practice. With discipline, perseverance, and the will to learn, a financially secure future is not only possible, but also probable. The journey towards financial freedom starts with a single step—take that step today.

Chapter 8. Investment Basics: Making Your Money Work for You

In every individual's financial journey, understanding investment basics plays a crucial role. Investment can be perceived as an intimidating concept for beginners, but it doesn't have to be. Bury the intimidation under a stern vow to learn and grow, and you'll find that the world beyond saved pennies and bank balances can lead to impressive financial potential. Embrace this world with a strategic approach to investment, and your money will respond positively by working for you and amplifying your wealth.

8.1. Understanding Investments

Investments refer to the process of putting your money or resources into an asset, fund, or project with the goal of earning returns over time. These could be assets like stocks, bonds, or real estate, investment funds such as mutual funds or Exchange Traded Funds (ETFs), or personal or business projects that can generate income or value.

Investments are an essential way to build wealth because they offer the possibility of returns over and above what could be earned through work or conventional saving alone. With the right investment strategy, it's possible to grow a modest sum into a significant wealth reserve.

8.2. Why Invest?

In the world where economic uncertainties exist, the role of savings cannot be underestimated. Yet, save alone, and your money loses purchasing power because of inflation, a scenario where price levels in an economy are increasing over time.

Without investing, your money doesn't grow—it only maintains. You need to actively scout for methods to make your money work for you. And that's where investment comes in. It harnesses the power of compounding, allows your money to generate more money by earning interest on the amount already earned, and provides possible higher returns than traditional savings.

8.3. Types of Investments

Investments come in various shapes and sizes. Depending on how hands-on you want to be to varying degrees of risk and potential returns, there are different investment groups suited for every individual investor.

Stocks

Stocks represent your ownership in a company. As a shareholder, you have a claim to part of the company's assets and earnings. Stocks are known for promising high returns but also, high risk. The stock market can be volatile, with prices rising and falling rapidly.

Bonds

Bonds are loans that you give to the government or a company. When you buy a bond, you provide the borrowed amount for a certain period, and in return, you'll receive the loan amount plus interest at maturity. Bonds are less risky than stocks but offer modest returns.

Mutual Funds and ETFs

Mutual funds and exchange-traded funds (ETFs) function like investment baskets. By buying a share of a mutual fund or an ETF, you're buying a basket of different investments. This setup allows you to diversify your investments easily.

Real Estate

Real estate involves purchasing property to earn income, either through rent or property appreciation. While it often requires a substantial amount initially, it can be a steady income source.

Other Investments

Besides these, there are myriad other investment forms, like commodities, Certificates of Deposit (CDs), retirement accounts such as 401(k) and IRAs, robo-advisors, and more. As you become more versed in investing, you may choose to explore these areas.

8.4. The Importance of Diversification

Regardless of which types of investments you choose, diversification is vital. It's an investment strategy to spread the risk among various investment classes. By not putting all your eggs in one basket, you limit your potential losses if one asset class takes a hit. Diversification can stabilize your portfolio, provide smoother investment returns, and lessen the impact of volatility.

8.5. Taking the First Steps in Investing

Getting started in investing can be daunting, but it's the first step towards growing your wealth effectively. Those who are new to the investment world might consider starting with low-risk investments, such as bonds or mutual funds, before gradually moving onto high-risk investments like stocks.

Note that sound investing requires understanding the finer intricacies of the investment landscape, a substantial amount of time for research, and continuous monitoring. Hence, many individuals may choose to work with a financial advisor.

8.6. Working With a Financial Advisor

A financial advisor is a professional who provides investment advice and helps build a personalized investment strategy. This relationship can be valuable, especially to those who are new to investing or prefer a more hands-on approach.

A good financial advisor will take into account your financial goals, risk tolerance, and investment horizon before suggesting a suitable investment strategy. They also regularly monitor your portfolio and adjust your investment plan as necessary.

8.7. ROI: Understanding Returns on Investments

An investment's return, or ROI, is the gain or loss made from an investment over a period. It is typically expressed as a percentage and can encompass both realized and unrealized gains and losses. Higher ROI means better investment performance.

However, remember that high rewards come with high risks. So, strive for balance. Diversify your portfolio to mitigate risk and achieve more stable returns.

In conclusion, while the investment landscape may seem vast at the moment, don't get deterred. With your dedication and tenacity, you can demystify and master investments, thereby getting your wealth to work for you. Here's to your money blossoming under the sunshine of financial wisdom!

Chapter 9. Risk Management: Insurance and Your Wealth

The first road to financial empowerment is understanding the value of risk management. Risk management is an essential pillar of personal finance, allowing you to safeguard your wealth during unforeseen circumstances. And one of the primary tools for managing risk is insurance. This chapter aims to give you an in-depth understanding of insurance and its vital role in managing your wealth.

9.1. Understanding Risk and the Need for Insurance

Risk is inherent in almost all aspects of our lives, including personal finance. It's the potential for a negative or undesirable outcome. As much as we do our best to avoid or mitigate them, unexpected incidents such as accidents, illnesses, and disasters, which carry significant financial implications, are inevitable. Here is where insurance steps in.

Essentially, insurance is a financial tool that allows you to pool your risks with others. By paying a regular premium to an insurance company, you can protect yourself from substantial financial losses. In the event of a covered incident, the insurance company bears the cost.

9.2. The Various Types of Insurances

Insurance isn't one-size-fits-all. There are mitigation tools for various aspects of life, ensuring that whatever your circumstances, there is likely coverage that fits your needs:

1. **Life Insurance**: This insurance compensates your dependents upon your death, providing them financial security.

2. **Health Insurance**: Health insurance covers medical expenses, from routine check-ups to hospital stays and surgical procedures.

3. **Disability Insurance**: This policy provides you with income if you become unable to work due to an injury or illness.

4. **Homeowner's Insurance**: Covers possible damages to your home, either due to natural disasters, theft, or other causes.

5. **Auto Insurance**: It's a legal requirement for drivers in most states and can safeguard against the financial implications of vehicular accidents.

6. **Liability Insurance**: If you're legally liable for an accident, this coverage can help protect your assets.

9.3. The Importance of Adequate Coverage

The purpose of insurance isn't just to have it; it's about having adequate coverage. Inadequate insurance can leave you exposed to risks that can erode your wealth. Regularly assess your needs to ensure your coverage is enough to protect your assets and provide for your dependents if necessary.

9.4. Evaluating Insurance Policies

Every insurance policy is different, and not all will suit your needs. Consider the following factors when evaluating an insurance policy:

1. **The Premium**: This is the cost for having the insurance plan. While it's crucial to find affordable insurance, the cheapest option might not provide adequate coverage.

2. **The Deductible**: This is the set amount you must pay before the

insurance coverage kicks in. A policy with a lower premium often has a higher deductible, and vice versa.

3. **Exclusions**: These are specific situations, conditions, or circumstances that are not covered by the policy.

4. **Limitations**: These are caps on the amount the insurance company will pay for certain types of claims. Be careful; some policies may have low limits that might not be sufficient in a catastrophic event.

9.5. Making Insurance Work for You

Insurance shouldn't be bought impulsively or simply because it's offered. Understand the terms of your policy, be aware of what's covered and what's not. And remember, insurance should be part of a larger financial plan, not an isolated product.

As you progress in your financial journey, your insurance needs will evolve. Carry out periodic reviews, adjust policies as necessary, and ensure each type of insurance integrates smoothly with the overall vision for your financial future.

Remember, mastering wealth isn't just about acquiring assets; it's also about protecting them. By thoroughly understanding the ins and outs of insurance, you can ensure that your financial future is secure, regardless of what life throws at you.

By making the smart decision today to understand and apply the principles of risk management, you make lenient the path to financial success and peace of mind, laying a secure foundation on which to pursue your dreams and goals. The beauty of insurance is that it grants peace of mind, secure in the knowledge that we are protected against the various risks that life might throw our way. This knowledge is a valuable addition to our powerhouse of financial wisdom.

Navigating the world of insurance can be complex, but the payoff—both tangible and intangible—is immense. The ability to protect and preserve the wealth you're working so hard to amass is priceless. Here's to taking one more step towards mastering your wealth through sound risk management.

In the next chapter, we will springboard off this foundation, diving into investment strategies that can help you grow and multiply your wealth in a way that aligns with your goals and risk tolerance.

Chapter 10. Planning for Retirement: Building Your Nest Egg

Early retirement plans may conjure images of endless vacations or dabbling in your favorite hobbies without the pressure of a nine-to-five routine. However, proper planning holds the keys to a successful and hassle-free retirement. Building your nest egg isn't an overnight achievement—it's a long-term commitment. This chapter will guide you through the fundamental strategies to ensure a relatively seamless transition into the golden years.

10.1. The Importance of Starting Early

At dinner parties or family gatherings, the subject of retirement planning might not sneak into the conversations, especially if you're in your 20s or 30s. Yet, it is crucial to start early. Why?

Compound interest serves as the magic ingredient turning your savings into monumental returns over the years. It feeds a cycle where the interest you earn on your savings is reinvested to earn more interest. Thus, time proves to be your greatest ally. Waiting until your 40s or 50s to start saving hinders your ability to fully exploit the power of compound interest.

It might be helpful to picture your future self, stepping into an unburdened retirement, and thank your present self for each penny set aside now. As the saying goes, "the best time to plant a tree was 20 years ago. The next best time is now."

10.2. Choosing the Right Retirement Plan

Understanding the retirement savings landscape is a critical step toward building a robust nest egg. Multiple retirement plans offer various features, and you should understand the implications of each. Here is a breakdown of common plans:

- **Traditional 401(k)**: Offered by many employers, 401(k) plans carry a benefit of pre-tax contributions. These plans often feature employer match programs, which effectively provide free money to your retirement savings. Be aware that withdrawals during retirement are taxed as regular income.

- **Roth 401(k)**: Like the traditional 401(k), many employers offer Roth 401(k) plans. The contribution occurs after taxes, meaning withdrawals during retirement aren't subject to additional tax. As a result, increasing income tax rates will not erode your savings later in life.

- **Individual Retirement Accounts (IRA)**: Many options exist under the umbrella of IRAs. Traditional and Roth IRAs work much like their 401(k) counterparts regarding tax treatments. There are also SEP IRAs for self-employed individuals or small business owners, offering higher contribution limits.

Choosing the right plan depends on various factors like your present income, tax rates, projected future income, the possibility of employer match, and the control you wish to exert over investments. It's wise to consult with a financial advisor to make an informed decision.

10.3. Diversification of Investments

Retirement accounts don't amplify wealth magically—they are vessels that hold a diversified portfolio of investments, ideally providing a balance between risk and reward. The common investment categories include:

- **Stocks**: They represent equity in a company, bringing potentially high rewards accompanied by substantial risk.

- **Bonds**: Bonds are loans provided to a company or government entity, repaid over time with interest. Generally, bonds come with lower risk than stocks but also provide lower returns.

- **Mutual funds**: These funds spread money across a mix of stocks, bonds, and other assets, managed by professional fund managers.

- **Real estate**: Offering an alternative to the stock market, real estate investment trusts (REITs) invest in property and can form part of a robust retirement portfolio.

Your individual risk tolerance, retirement timeline, and financial goals contribute to your ideal asset allocation. Diversification remains a cornerstone strategy, spreading your investments across asset classes that are not closely correlated to ride out market fluctuations.

10.4. Calculating Your Retirement Needs

Predicting future financial needs during retirement can feel like chasing a moving target due to factors like inflation, unforeseen healthcare costs, or changes in living expenses. Some financial advisors suggest a retirement income of about 70% to 80% of your pre-retirement salary. Yet, specific circumstances may dictate higher or lower needs.

To map out a rough estimate of your required nest egg, consider the following steps:

1. Calculate your current expenses and adjust them based on

expected lifestyle changes during retirement.

2. Subtract estimated post-retirement incomes (like Social Security, pensions, annuities, or part-time work incomes) from the adjusted expenses.

3. Allow for inflation. You can estimate an average inflation rate of 2% to 3% annually.

4. Calculate the total retirement corpus needed using a safe withdrawal rate. A common rate is 4%; although, it could vary.

Remember, it's better to overestimate and adjust later than underestimate and face a financial crunch during your retirement years.

10.5. Regular Monitoring and Adjustments

Your retirement planning journey won't be set in stone. Life events like marriage, the birth of a child, job changes, or unexpected health issues can impact your financial landscape. Regularly reviewing your strategy and making necessary adjustments will help you stay on track.

Annually revisiting your retirement accounts to rebalance and realign them with your financial objectives is good practice. Factors like changes in income, risk tolerance, or nearing retirement might require shifts in your investment strategy.

As retirement nears, typically, the focus should shift from accumulating wealth to preserving it. This transition necessitates reallocation of assets from riskier investments like stocks to safer ones like bonds.

Takeaway: Planning for retirement means more than putting away a tiny fraction of your income each month—it's a strategic, personal plan. By understanding your current financial landscape, predicting future needs, and maintaining vigilance on your plan, you can build a nest egg to secure a comfortable retirement. As with any complicated journey, the road to successful retirement involves patience, discipline, and sometimes, the wisdom of experienced financial advisors.

Chapter 11. Estate Planning: Safeguarding Your Wealth

Estate planning is about ensuring that your wealth, accumulated over a lifetime of earning, saving, and investing, reaches its due beneficiaries as per your wishes. It is about preserving, growing, and transferring your wealth in the most effective, tax-efficient manner. It is about planning for the unforeseen, having your desires addressed, and making sure your loved ones aren't burdened with uncertainty in tough times.

11.1. The Basics of Estate Planning

An estate comprises everything you own— your car, home, other real estate, checking and savings accounts, investments, life insurance, furniture, personal belongings. Regardless of age, or the size of your estate, an estate plan can ensure the right people inherit your possessions. Without one, the authorities could take control of the distribution process, which may not align with your preferences.

Estate plans typically include wills, trusts, health care directives, power of attorney agreements, and other relevant documents. It is important to update these regularly as investment portfolios grow and life circumstances change. Different approaches apply depending on marital status, age, and wealth level, so let's break it down.

11.2. Importance of a Will

A will, a legal document, dictates how you desire your assets to be distributed after your death. A sizeable chunk of individuals, across all income brackets, don't have a will and the consequences can be quite drastic.

Without a will, your estate is distributed according to the laws of intestacy, and the state decides who gets what. This can be a long-drawn, exhausting process, and the outcome may not adhere to your wishes. Furthermore, a will allows you to select a guardian for minor children.

If you die without a will (intestate), a court will choose guardians for your children. A good rule of thumb is to make a will while you're young and revise it every five years, or as required by changes in your life circumstances.

11.3. Setting up Trusts

Trusts are not merely for the wealthy; they can be useful for people of modest means as well. Two primary types of trusts are used in estate planning: revocable (living) trusts and irrevocable trusts.

A revocable trust can be altered or canceled at any time by the grantor. Assets within these trusts bypass the probate process, providing confidentiality and speeding asset distribution to beneficiaries.

Irrevocable trusts cannot be changed without permission from the beneficiary. These trusts provide tax advantages by removing taxable assets from the estate. By forming a trust, you can designate a trustee to manage and distribute your assets on behalf of your beneficiaries as per your stipulations.

It is important to remember that establishing trusts can be complex. Always enlist the services of an experienced estate planning attorney to ensure that trusts align with your overall financial plan.

11.4. Health Care Directives and Power of Attorney

Health care directives, also known as living wills, outline your wishes regarding end-of-life care. Should you become incapacitated and unable to make decisions, these directives will dictate your treatment.

A power of attorney is another critical component of your estate plan. This legal document allows you to appoint a trusted individual to handle your financial affairs if you become incapacitated. Without a power of attorney, a court proceeding may be required to appoint a guardian or conservator to act on your behalf.

11.5. Estate Tax Planning

Estate tax can take a significant bite out of your estate's wealth. Proactive estate tax planning can assist you in leaving more of your assets to your beneficiaries and less to the taxman. This includes strategies such as unlimited marital deduction, annual gifting, charitable donations, setting up trusts, and life insurance planning. Work with a qualified financial advisor to formulate an estate tax plan that fits your needs.

11.6. Regularly Review and Update Your Plan

Estate planning is not a one-and-done event; it requires regular upkeep as personal circumstances and laws evolve. Reviewing your estate plan regularly ensures that it stays all-weather ready and reflective of your current wishes. Make it a habit to review your plan at least once every two years or after significant events such as births, deaths, marriages, or divorces.

In conclusion, estate planning secures your wealth and ensures a smooth transition of assets to your loved ones. It's more than just writing a will—it's about making wise decisions that protect both your assets and your loved ones. With structured planning and regular reviews, you can have peace of mind knowing your legacy is protected.

Remember, there are no universal estate planning solutions. An effective plan is tailored to your personal situation, preferences, and changes over time. So, it's time to take the first steps towards safeguarding your wealth through comprehensive estate planning. Your future self, and your descendants, will be thankful you did.

www.ingramcontent.com/pod-product-compliance
Lightning Source LLC
Chambersburg PA
CBHW062305290526
45794CB00006B/2698